HONEY AND SALT

By CARL SANDBURG

Abraham Lincoln: The Prairie Years (*Two Volumes*), 1926
Abraham Lincoln: The War Years (*Four Volumes*), 1939
Abraham Lincoln: The Prairie Years and The War Years
(*One-Volume Edition*), 1954
The Chicago Race Riots, 1919
The American Songbag, 1927
Steichen the Photographer, 1929
Potato Face, 1930
Mary Lincoln: Wife and Widow (*documented by Paul M. Angle*), 1932
Storm Over the Land, 1942
Home Front Memo, 1943
The Photographs of Abraham Lincoln (*with Frederick H. Meserve*), 1944
Lincoln Collector: The Story of the Oliver R. Barrett Lincoln Collection, 1949
Always the Young Strangers, 1953
The Sandburg Range, 1957

NOVEL

Remembrance Rock, 1948

POETRY

Chicago Poems, 1916
Cornhuskers, 1918
Smoke and Steel, 1920
Slabs of the Sunburnt West, 1922
Selected Poems (*edited by Rebecca West*), 1926
Good Morning, America, 1928
The People, Yes, 1936
Complete Poems, 1950
Harvest Poems: 1910-1960, 1960

FOR YOUNG FOLKS

Rootabaga Stories, 1922
Rootabaga Pigeons, 1923
Abe Lincoln Grows Up, 1928
Early Moon, 1930
Prairie-Town Boy, 1955
Wind Song, 1960

HONEY AND SALT

CARL SANDBURG

HARCOURT, BRACE & WORLD, INC.　　NEW YORK

CONTENTS

19245

HONEY AND SALT

HONEY AND SALT

A bag of tricks—is it?
   And a game smoothies play?
If you're good with a deck of cards
or rolling the bones—that helps?
If you can tell jokes and be a chum
and make an impression—that helps?
When boy meets girl or girl meets boy—
                what helps?
They all help: be cozy but not too cozy:
be shy, bashful, mysterious, yet only so-so:
then forget everything you ever heard about love
for it's a summer tan and a winter windburn
and it comes as weather comes and you can't change it:
it comes like your face came to you, like your legs came
and the way you walk, talk, hold your head and hands—
and nothing can be done about it—you wait and pray.
   Is there any way of measuring love?
   Yes but not till long afterward
     when the beat of your heart has gone
     many miles, far into the big numbers.
Is the key to love in passion, knowledge, affection?
All three—along with moonlight, roses, groceries,
givings and forgivings, gettings and forgettings,
     keepsakes and room rent,
     pearls of memory along with ham and eggs.
Can love be locked away and kept hid?
     Yes and it gathers dust and mildew
     and shrivels itself in shadows
     unless it learns the sun can help,
     snow, rain, storms can help—
     birds in their one-room family nests
     shaken by winds cruel and crazy—
     they can all help:
     lock not away your love nor keep it hid.

How comes the first sign of love?
In a chill, in a personal sweat,
in a you-and-me, us, us two,
in a couple of answers,
an amethyst haze on the horizon,
two dance programs criss-crossed,
jackknifed initials interwoven,
five fresh violets lost in sea salt,
birds flying at single big moments
in and out a thousand windows,
a horse, two horses, many horses,
a silver ring, a brass cry,
a golden gong going ong ong ong-ng-ng,
pink doors closing one by one
to sunset nightsongs along the west,
shafts and handles of stars,
folds of moonmist curtains,
winding and unwinding wisps of fogmist.

How long does love last?
As long as glass bubbles handled with care
or two hot-house orchids in a blizzard
or one solid immovable steel anvil
tempered in sure inexorable welding—
or again love might last as
six snowflakes, six hexagonal snowflakes,
six floating hexagonal flakes of snow
or the oaths between hydrogen and oxygen
in one cup of spring water
or the eyes of bucks and does
or two wishes riding on the back of a
morning wind in winter
or one corner of an ancient tabernacle
held sacred for personal devotions
or dust   yes   dust in a little solemn heap
played on by changing winds.

There are sanctuaries
          holding honey and salt.
There are those who
          spill and spend.
There are those who
          search and save.
And love may be a quest
          with silence and content.
Can you buy love?
Sure   every day with money, clothes, candy,
with promises, flowers, big-talk,
with laughter, sweet-talk, lies,
every day men and women buy love
and take it away and things happen
          and they study about it
          and the longer they look at it
the more it isn't love they bought at all:
          bought love is a guaranteed imitation.

          Can you sell love?
Yes   you can sell it and take the price
          and think it over
          and look again at the price
          and cry and cry to yourself
and wonder who was selling what and why.
Evensong lights floating black night waters,
a lagoon of stars washed in velvet shadows,
a great storm cry from white sea-horses—
          these moments cost beyond all prices.

          Bidden or unbidden? how comes love?
Both bidden and unbidden, a sneak and a shadow,
          a dawn in a doorway throwing a dazzle
          or a sash of light in a blue fog,

a slow blinking of two red lanterns in river mist
or a deep smoke winding one hump of a mountain
and the smoke becomes a smoke known to your own
        twisted individual garments:
the winding of it gets into your walk, your hands,
        your face and eyes.

PASS, FRIEND

The doors of the morning must open.
The keys of the night are not thrown away.

I who have loved morning know its doors.
I who have loved night know its keys.

ALONE AND NOT ALONE

I

There must be a place
a room and a sanctuary
set apart for silence
for shadows and roses
holding aware in walls
the sea and its secrets
gong clamor gone still
in a long deep sea-wash
aware always of gongs
vanishing before shadows
of roses repeating themes
of ferns standing still
till wind blows over them:
great hunger may bring these
into one little room
set apart for silence

II

There must be substance here
related to old communions of
hungering men and women—
brass is a hard lean metal
gold is the most ductile metal—
they speak to each other not often
they melt and fuse
only in the crucible of this communion
only in the dangers of high moments—
they moan as mist before wind

8

The shuttlings of dawn color go soft
weaving out of the night of black ice
with crimson ramblers
up the latticed ladders of daytime arriving.
The riders of the sea   the long white horses
they send their plungers obedient to the moon
in a dedicated path of foam and rainbows.
The praise of any slow red moonrise should be slow.
There are storm winds who bow down to nothing.
They go on relentless under command and release
sent out to do their hammering whirls of storm.
There are sunset flames inviting prayer and sharing.
There are timepieces having silence between chimes.
Children of the wind keep their childish ways.
The wisps of blue in a smoke wreath are mortal.
The keepers of wisdom testify a heap of ashes
means whatever was there went out burning.

WINGTIP

The birds—are they worth remembering?
Is flight a wonder and one wingtip a
space marvel?
When will man know what birds know?

LOVE IS A DEEP AND A DARK AND A LONELY

love is a deep and a dark and a lonely
and you take it deep take it dark
and take it with a lonely winding
and when the winding gets too lonely
then may come the windflowers
and the breath of wind over many flowers
winding its way out of many lonely flowers
waiting in rainleaf whispers
waiting in dry stalks of noon
wanting in a music of windbreaths
so you can take love as it comes keening
as it comes with a voice and a face
and you make a talk of it
talking to yourself a talk worth keeping
and you put it away for a keen keeping
and you find it to be a hoarding
and you give it away and yet it stays hoarded

like a book read over and over again
like one book being a long row of books
like leaves of windflowers bending low
and bending to be never broken

ALMANAC

Scrutinize the Scorpion constellation
and see where a hook of stars
ends with a lonely star.

Go to the grey sea horizon
and ask for a message
and listen and wait.

See whether the conundrums
of a heavy land fog
either sing or talk.

Let only a small cry come
in behalf of a clean sunrise:
the sun performs so often.

Speak to the branches of spring
and the surprise of blossoms:
they too hope for a good year.

Search the first winter snowstorm
for a symphonic arrangement:
it is always there.

Take an alphabet of gold or mud and spell
as you wish any words: kiss me, kill me,
love, hate, ice, thought, victory.

Read the numbers on your wrist watch
and ask: is being born, being loved,
being dead, nothing but numbers?

BIOGRAPHY

A biography, sirs, should begin—with the breath of a man
when his eyes first meet the light of day—then working on
through to the death when the light of day is gone:
so the biography then is finished—unless you reverse the order
and begin with the death and work back to the birth—
starting the life with a coffin, moving back to a cradle—
in which case, sirs, the biography has arrived, is completed
when you have your subject born, except for ancestry, lineage,
forbears, pedigree, blood, breed, bones, backgrounds—
and these, sirs, may be carried far.

ANECDOTE OF HEMLOCK FOR TWO ATHENIANS

The grizzled Athenian ordered to hemlock,
Ordered to a drink and lights out,
Had a friend he never refused anything.

"Let me drink too," the friend said.
And the grizzled Athenian answered,
"I never yet refused you anything."

"I am short of hemlock enough for two,"
The head executioner interjected,
"There must be more silver for more hemlock."

"Somebody pay this man for the drinks of death,"
The grizzled Athenian told his friends,
Who fished out the ready cash wanted.

"Since one cannot die on free cost at Athens,
Give this man his money," were the words
Of the man named Phocion, the grizzled Athenian.

Yes, there are men who know how to die in a grand way.
There are men who make their finish worth mentioning.

DREAMING FOOL

I was the first of the fools
(So I dreamed)
And all the fools of the world
    were put into me and I was
    the biggest fool of all.

Others were fools in the morning
Or in the evening or on Saturdays
Or odd days like Friday the Thirteenth
But me—I was a fool every day in the week
And when asleep I was the sleeping fool.
(So I dreamed.)

LIEF THE LUCKY

Lief Ericson crossed the sea
to get away from a woman—
did he?

I have looked deep into the cisterns of the stars—
said Lief—and the stars too, every one was a struggler.

My neck shall not be broken without a little battle—
said Lief—and I shall always sing a little in tough weather.

I hunted alligators on the moon and they had excellent teeth
for grinding even as the camels had excellent humps
for humping—so ran one of his dreams.

He told the crew of a souse who said, Get me drunk and have some
fun with me—and his mood changed and he told them it
would be grand to travel the sky in a chariot of fire
like Elijah.

He saw a soft milk white horse on the top cone of an iceberg
looking for a place to slide down to pearl purple sea
foam—and he murmured, "I've been lonely too, though
never so lonely one wind wouldn't take me home to the
four winds."

He went on murmuring, "Never have I known time to fail me,
time with its monotonous mumbling in the masts and
stanchions, its plashing plashing measuring plashing
to the bulwarks, the slinking of the sea after a storm,
the crying of the birds as they ride the wind when the
wind goes down."

He lifted his head toward scrawny warning horizons and nailed
up a slogan: Blessed are they who expect nothing for
they shall not be disappointed:

Yes Lief Ericson crossed the sea
to get away from a woman—
perhaps—maybe.

BIRD FOOTPRINT

The footprint of a bird in sand brought your face.
I said, "What of it?"

And the next lone footprint of a bird in the sand
brought your face again.
I said, "It is written deeper than sand."

I saw a bird wing fixed forty thousand years in a rock,
a bird wing bringing your foot, your wrist.

CAHOKIA

The Indian saw the butterfly
rise out of the cocoon.
That was enough for him.
The butterfly had wings, freedom.

The Indian saw flowers in spring
push up out of the ground.
He saw the rain and the thunder.
They were enough for him.

And he saw the sun.
But he didn't worship the sun.
For him the sun was a sign, a symbol.
He bowed in prayer to what was behind the sun.
He made songs and dances to the makers and movers
    of the sun.

BUYERS AND SELLERS

What is a man worth?
What can he do?
What is his value?
On the one hand those who buy labor,
On the other hand those who have nothing
    to sell but their labor.
And when the buyers of labor tell the
    sellers, "Nothing doing today, not a
    chance!"—then what?

CITY NUMBER

The soiled city oblongs stand sprawling.
The blocks and house numbers go miles.
Trucks howl rushing the early morning editions.
Night-club dancers have done their main floor show.
Tavern trios improvise "Show me the way to go home."
Soldiers and sailors look for street corners, house numbers.
Night watchmen figure halfway between midnight and breakfast.
Look out the window now late after the evening that was.
    On a south sky of pigeon-egg blue
    Long clouds float in a silver moonbath.

CHROMO

This old river town saw the
early steamboats.
The line of wharf and houses
is a faded chromo.
It is bleached and bitten standing
to steady sunrises.

THE EVENING SUNSETS WITNESS AND PASS ON

Passion may call for a partner
to share the music of its bones,
to weave shadows, rain, moonshine, dreams—
Passion may hammer on hard door panels,
empty a hot vocabulary of wanting, wanting—
it is all there in the fragments of Sappho.

Passion may consider poppies cheap
with their strong stalks in the wind,
with their crying crimson sheaths—
Passion may remember tiger lilies,
keepers of a creeping evening mist,
tawny watchers of the morning stars—
Passion may cry to the moon
for miracles of flesh,
for red answers to a white riddle—
it is told in the tears on many love letters.

Passion may spend its money,
its youth, its laughter, all else,
till again passion is alone
spending its cries to the moon—
and some weep, some sing, some go to war.
Passion may be alone at a window
seeing kisses fasten lips in wild troths,
a storm of red silk scarfs in a high wind,
armfuls of redbirds let loose into bush and sky—
and some weep, some sing, some go to war.

Passion may come with baskets
throwing paths of red rain flowers,
each folded petal a sacrament—
the evening sunsets witness and pass on.

Passion may build itself houses of air
and look from a thousand tall windows—
till the wind rides and gathers.

Passion may be a wind child
transient and made of air—
Passion may be a wild grass
where a great wind came and went.

The evening sunsets witness and pass on.

DEEP SEA WANDERING

deep sea was the wandering
deep brass the dripping loot
deep crimson the bloodspill
lyrics begotten on lush lips
and many a hawser they saw
rotting rope and rusting chain
and anchors   many lost anchors

CALL THE NEXT WITNESS

there will be people left over
enough inhabitants among the Eskimos
among jungle folk
denizens of plains and plateaus
cities and towns synthetic miasma missed
enough for a census
enough to call it still a world
though definitely   my friends   my good friends
definitely not the same old world
the vanquished saying, "What happened?"
the victors saying, "We planned it so."
if it should be at the end
in the smoke   the mist   the silence of the end
if it should be one side lost   the other side won

the changes among these leftover people
the scattered ones the miasma missed
their programs of living   their books and music
they will be simple and conclusive
in the ways and manners of early men and women
the children having playroom
rulers and diplomats finding affairs less complex
new types of cripples here and there
and indescribable babbling survivors
listening to plain scholars saying,
should a few plain scholars have come through,
"As after other wars the peace is something else again."

amid the devastated areas and the untouched
the historians will take an interest
finding amid the ruins and shambles
tokens of contrast and surprise
testimonies here curious   there monstrous
nuclear-fission corpses having one face

radioactivity cadavers another look
bacteriological victims not unfamiliar
scenes and outlooks nevertheless surpassing
      those of the First World War
      and those of the Second or Global War
      —the historians will take an interest
      fill their note-books   pick their way
      amid burned and tattered documents
      and say to each other,
      "What the hell! it isn't worth writing,
      posterity won't give a damn what we write."

EARLY COPPER

A slim and singing copper girl,
They lived next to the earth for her sake
And the yellow corn was in their faces
And the copper curve of prairie sunset.

   In her April eyes bringing
Corn tassels shining from Duluth and Itasca,
From La Crosse to Keokuk and St. Louis, to the Big Muddy,
The yellow-hoofed Big Muddy meeting the Father of Waters,
In her eyes corn rows running to the prairie ends,
In her eyes copper men living next to the earth for her sake.

ATLAS, HOW HAVE YOU BEEN?

The shape of the world is either a box or a bag
and a box-shaped world has corners
and a bag-shaped world is either open or closed
and Somebody holds the bag.

Now whether the world is oblong, square or rhomboid
or whether the world is a series of circles,
rings twisted into each other's eternal grooves,
or whether the world keeps changing from box to bag,
from corners to circles and back to corners,
from rings to oblongs and back to rings
and repeating the twist into the groove
and practicing that twist over again
from box to bag and bag again to box—
this was what we were talking about
when the first thunder crashed
and lightning forked across a black rain.

We decided the earth itself isn't much.
It is mapped and measured now
And we fly around it in just a few breakfasts.
And the strong man they named Atlas
Should have had that very name of Atlas
If he had stood under the earth ball
And held it on his big shoulders.
Atlas, you were made as a make-believe
And we give you a make-believe salute.
We say: Atlas, how are you doing,
                    how have you been?

Beyond the ball of earth are other balls,
also double balls, triple balls, series of balls,
and balloons, drums, cylinders, triangles, jugs,
some with handles identified and signed,

others with anonymous sprockets and axles—
and we decided amid the sheet lightning—
the whole works is held either in a box or a bag,
afterwards asking ourselves:
what is outside the box, what props up the bag?
these are big questions, we told each other
while sprags of lightning dropped from the sky—
clutches and magnets, clocks and wheels
made of a mud and air beyond our dreams,
ordered in verbs beyond our doorways.

We decided at last
the world might be a box when awake
and a bag when asleep
and while we slept
it changed from box to bag
and back from bag to box
and the forgetfulness of our own sleep
is strange and beautiful by itself
and sometimes in its shifting shapes
the world is a cradle dedicated to sleep
and what would you rather have than sleep?

CHEAP RENT

The laws of the bronze gods
are irrevocable.

And yet—in the statue of
General Grant astride a horse
on rolling prairie, on little
hills looking from Lincoln
Park at Lake Michigan—
here the sparrows have a nest
in General Grant's spy glass—
here the sparrows have rented
a flat in General Grant's
right stirrup—

It is true? The laws of the
bronze gods are irrevocable?

ELM BUDS

Elm buds are out.
Yesterday morning, last night,
    they crept out.
They are the mice of early
    spring air.

To the north is the gray sky.
Winter hung it gray for the gray
    elm to stand dark against.
Now the branches all end with the
    yellow and gold mice of early
    spring air.
They are moving mice creeping out
    with leaf and leaf.

CHILD FACE

There are lips as strange and soft
As a rim of moon many miles off,
White on a fading purple sea.
"Was it there, far-off, real,
Or did my eyes play me a trick?"

A finger can be laid across it,
Laid on a little mouth's white yearning,
Only as a white rim of moon
Can be picked off a blue sea
And sent in a love letter.

Once a child face lay in the moonlight
Of an early spring night.

FOG NUMBERS

Birth is the starting point of passion.
Passion is the beginning of death.
How can you turn back from birth?
How can you say no to passion?
How can you bid death hold off?
And if thoughts come and hold you
And if dreams step in and shake your bones
What can you do but take them and make them
       more your own?

    Of course, a nickel is a nickel,
    and a dime is a dime—sure—
    we learned that—
    why mention it now?
    of course, steel is steel;
    and a hammer is a hammer;
And a thought, a dream, is more than a name,
    a number, a fixed point.

      . .

Walk in a midnight fog now and say to it: Tell
    me your number and I'll tell mine.
Salute one morning sun falling on a river ribbon
    of mist and tell it: My number is such-and-
    such—what's yours?

Of what is fog the starting point?
Of what is the red sun the beginning?
Long ago—as now—little men and women knew in
    their bones the singing and the aching of
    these stumbling questions.

EVENING QUESTIONS

The swath of light climbs up the skyscraper
Around the corners of white prisms and spikes.
The inside torso stands up in a plug of gun-metal.
The shadow struggles to get loose from the light.
Shall I say I'm through and it's no use?
Or have I got another good fight in me?

FIFTY-FIFTY

What is there for us two
to split fifty-fifty,
to go halvers on?
    A Bible, a deck of cards?
    a farm, a frying pan?
    a porch, front steps to sit on?
How can we be pals
    when you speak English
    and I speak English
    and you never understand me
    and I never understand you?

EVENING SEA WIND

A molten gold flows away from the sun
to fall as a shingle of gold and glass
on waters holding five ships, a quintet,
five, no less, five sheathed in brass haze.
     On a bronze and copper path just over
     comes a maroon, comes a dusk of gun-metal.
A white horse shape of a moving cloud
meets a wind changing it to a small lamb,
meets a wind smoothing what it meets,
smoothing the lamb into six white snakes,
smoothing the snakes to a ball of wool.
     The sungold shingle, ships in brass haze
     fade into walls of umber, pools of ink
     and there is abbadabra and abracadabra.
     Two smoke rings, two nightmist bracelets
     seem to be telling us and themselves:
     "We blend and go, then again
          blend and go."

FORGOTTEN WARS

Be loose. Be easy. Be ready.
Forget the last war.
Forget the one before.
Forget the one yet to come.

Be loose and easy about the wars
whether they have been fought
or whether yet to be fought—
be ready to forget them.

Who was saying at high noon today:
"Is not each of them a forgotten war
after it is fought and over?
how and why it came forgotten?
how and what it cost forgotten?"
and was he there at Iwo Jima, Okinawa
or places named Cassino, Anzio, the Bulge?
and saying now:

"Let the next war before it comes
and before it gets under way
and five or six days sees its finish
or fifty years sees it still going strong
—let it be now a forgotten war.
        Be ready now to forget it.
        Be loose, be easy now.
The next war goes over in a flash—or runs long."

GOD IS NO GENTLEMAN

God gets up in the morning
    and says, "Another day?"
God goes to work every day
    at regular hours.
God is no gentleman for God
    puts on overalls and gets
    dirty running the universe we know
    about and several other universes
    nobody knows about but Him.

HUNGER AND COLD

Hunger long gone holds little heroic
to the hungering.

You don't eat and you get so you don't
care to eat nor ever remember eating—
and hearing of people who eat or don't
eat is all the same to you when you've
learned to keep your mind off eating
and eaters.

You become with enough hunger
the same as a tree with sap long gone
            or a dry leaf ready to fall.

Cold is cold and too cold is too cold.

The colder you get the more numb you get
and when you get numb enough you begin
to feel snug and cozy with warmth.

When the final numb glow of comfort goes
through you, then comes your slow smooth
slide into being frozen stiff and stark.

Then comes your easy entry at the tall
gates beyond which you are proof against
            ice or fire
            or tongues of malice
            or itch of ambition
or any phase of the peculiar torment known
            as unrequited love.

FOXGLOVES

Your heart was handed over
to the foxgloves one hot summer afternoon.
The snowsilk buds nodded and hung drowsy.
   So the stalks believed
   As they held those buds above.
   In deep wells of white
The dark fox fingers go in these gloves.
   In a slow fold of summer
Your heart was handed over in a curve
   from bud to bloom.

HARVEST

When the corn stands yellow in September,
A red flower ripens and shines among the stalks
And a red silk creeps among the broad ears
And tall tassels lift over all else
                    and keep a singing
                    to the prairies
                    and the wind.

          They are the grand lone ones
          For they are never saved
                    along with the corn:

                    They are cut down
                    and piled high
                    and burned.

                    Their fire
                    lights the west in November.

FAME IF NOT FORTUNE

A half-dollar in the hand of a gypsy
   tells me this and more:
You shall go broken on the wheel,
     lashed to the bars and fates of steel,
     a nickel's worth of nothing,
     a vaudeville gag,
     a child's busted rubber balloon kicked
        amid dirty bunting and empty popcorn
        bags at a summer park.
Yet cigarmakers shall name choice Havanas and
   paste your picture on the box,
Racehorses foaming under scarlet and ochre jockeys
   shall wear your name,
And policemen direct strangers to parks and schools
   remembered after you.

IMPASSE

Bring on a pail of smoke.
Bring on a sieve of coffee.
Bring on shovels speaking Javanese.
Open your newest, latest handkerchief
And let down a red-mouthed hankering hippopotamus.
Perform for us these offertories in blue.
Tell us again: Nothing is impossible.
We listen while you tell us.

IS WISDOM A LOT OF LANGUAGE?

Apes, may I speak to you a moment?
Chimpanzees, come hither for words.
Orangoutangs, let's get into a huddle.
Baboons, lemme whisper in your ears.
Gorillas, do yuh hear me hollerin' to yuh?
And monkeys! monkeys! get this chatter—

    For a long time men have plucked letters
    Out of the air and shaped syllables.
    And out of the syllables came words
    And from the words came phrases, clauses.
    Sentences were born—and languages.
    (The Tower of Babel didn't work out—
    it came down quicker than it went up.)
    Misunderstandings followed the languages,
    Arguments, epithets, maledictions, curses,
    Gossip, backbiting, the buzz of the bazoo,
    Chit chat, blah blah, talk just to be talking,
    Monologues of members telling other members
    How good they are now and were yesterday,
    Conversations missing the point,
    Dialogues seldom as beautiful as soliloquies,
    Seldom as fine as a man alone, a woman by herself
    Telling a clock, "I'm a plain damn fool."

Read the dictionary from A to Izzard today.
Get a vocabulary. Brush up on your diction.
See whether wisdom is just a lot of language.

KEEPSAKE BOXES

Now we shall open boxes and look.
In this one a storm was locked up, hoarse
    from long howling.
In this one lay fair weather, a blue sky
    manuscript.
In this one unfolded a gray monotone of
    a fog afternoon.
In each box was a day and its story of
    air and wind.
Sometimes one shook with confusions,
    processionals of weather.
"One day may be too much to gather, consider,
    and look among keepsakes."

: :

IMPOSSIBLE IAMBICS

He saw a fire dancer take two flambeaus
And do red shadows with her shoulders.
And he met two fools looking on and saying
Horsefeathers horsefeathers, and he said
I must bethink myself, I must throw seven
Eleven, O God am I a two-spot or what am
I? a who or a what or a which am I?
        And the next day it rained,
        the next day was something
        else again.

Well, hibiscus, what would you?
The flambeau dancer did it,
        she and the red shadows she threw.

LACKAWANNA TWILIGHT

Twilight and little mountain
towns along the Lehigh, sundown
and grey lavender flush.

Miners with dinner buckets and
headlamps, state constabulary on
horses, guns in holsters, Scranton,
Wilkesbarre, the Lackawanna Trail.

Twilight and the blessed armistice
of late afternoon and early evening.

Twilight and the sport sheets, movies,
chain programs, magazines, comics,
revival meetings.
Twilight and headlights on the new
hard roads, boy friend and girl friend,
dreams, romance, bread, wages, babies,
homes.

IF SO HAP MAY BE

Be somber with those in smoke garments.
Laugh with those eating bitter weeds.
Burn your love with bold flame blossoms,
      if so hap may be.
Leave him with a soft snowfall memory,
      if so hap may be.

            · ·

    Never came winter stars more clear
    yet the stars lost themselves
    midnight came snow-wrought snow-blown.

            · ·

KISSES, CAN YOU COME BACK LIKE GHOSTS?

If we ask you to gleam through the tears,
Kisses, can you come back like ghosts?

Today, tomorrow, the gateways take them.
"Always some door eats my shadow."

Love is a clock and the works wear out.
Love is a violin and the wood rots.
Love is a day with night at the end.
Love is a summer with falltime after.
Love dies always and when it dies it is dead
And when it is dead there is nothing more to it
And when there is nothing more to it then we say
This is the end, it comes always, it came to us.
And now we will bury it and put it away
Beautifully and decently, like a clock or a violin,
Like a summer day near falltime,
Like any lovely thing brought to the expected end.

Yes, let it go at that.
The clock rang and we answered.
The moon swept an old valley.
And we counted all of its rings.
The water-birds flipped in the river
And flicked their wing-points in sunset gold.
To the moon and the river water-birds,
To these we answered as the high calls rang.
And now? Now we take the clock and put it away.
Now we count again the rings of the valley moon
        and put them away as keepsakes.

Now we count the river-birds once more and let
  them slip loose and slip up the valley curve.
This is the end, there is always an end.

   Kisses, can you
   come back
       like ghosts?

LAKE MICHIGAN MORNING

Blue and white came out,
Riders of an early fall morning,
The blue by itself, the white by itself.

A young lamb white
crossed on a clear water blue.
Blue rollers talked on a beach white sand.
Water blown from snowwhite mountains
met the blue rise of lowland waters.

This was an early morning of high price.
    Blue bowls of white water
Poured themselves into white bowls of blue water.
There was a back-and-forth and a kiss-me kill-me
    washing and weaving.

NEW WEATHER

Mist came up as a man's hand.
Fog lifted as a woman's shawl.
Fair weather rode in with a blue oath.
One large cloud bellied in a white wind.
Two new winds joined for weather.
Splinters of rain broke out of the west.
Blue rains soaked in a lowland loam.
The dahlia leaves are points of red.
Bees roam singing in the buckwheat.
Russet and gold are the wheatstraws.
Forgotten bells fade and change.
Forgetful bells fill the air.
Fog shawls and mist hands come again.
New weather weaves new garments.

LESSON

In early April the trees
end their winter waiting
with a creep of green on branches.

::

In early October the trees
listen for a wind crying,
for leaves whirling.

::

The face of the river by night
holds a scatter of stars
and the silence of summer blossoms
falling to the moving water.

::

Come clean with a child heart.
Laugh as peaches in the summer wind.
Let rain on a house roof be a song.
Let the writing on your face
       be a smell of apple orchards in late June.

::

METAMORPHOSIS

When water turns ice does it remember
one time it was water?
When ice turns back into water does it
remember it was ice?

LOVE BEYOND KEEPING

She had a box
with a million red silk bandannas for him.
She gave them to him
one by one or by thousands,
saying then she had not enough for him.

She had languages and landscapes
on her lips and the end of her tongue,
landscapes of sunny hills and changing fogs,
of houses falling and people within falling,
of a left-handed man
who died for a woman who went out of her mind,
of a guitar player
who died with fingers reaching for strings,
of a man whose heart stopped
as his hand went out to put a pawn forward
on the fifth day of one game of chess,
of five gay women
stricken and lost
amid the javelins and chants
of love beyond keeping.

MOODS

The same gold of summer was on the winter hills,
the oat straw gold, the gold of slow sun change.

The stubble was chilly and lonesome,
the stub feet clomb up the hills and stood.

The flat cry of one wheeling crow faded and came,
ran on the stub gold flats and faded and came.

Fade-me, find-me, slow lights rang their changes
on the flats of oat straw gold on winter hills.

::

Use your skypiece.
Let the works of your noggin run.
Try one way, try another, throw away
    and throw away, junk your first,
    your second, junk sixty-six.
Keep your skypiece going, your noggin
    running, sit with your eyes shut
    and your thumbs quiet as two
    sleeping mice.

MOON RONDEAU

"Love is a door we shall open together."
So they told each other under the moon
One evening when the smell of leaf mould
And the beginnings of roses and potatoes
Came on a wind.

Late in the hours of that evening
They looked long at the moon and called it
A silver button, a copper coin, a bronze wafer,
A plaque of gold, a vanished diadem,
A brass hat dripping from deep waters.

   "People like us,
    us two,
   We own the moon."

LITTLE WORD, LITTLE WHITE BIRD

Love, is it a cat with claws and wild mate screams
  in the black night?
Love, is it a bird—a goldfinch with a burnish
  on its wingtips or a little gray sparrow
  picking crumbs, hunting crumbs?
Love, is it a tug at the heart that comes high and
  costs, always costs, as long as you have it?
Love, is it a free glad spender, ready to spend to
  the limit, and then go head over heels in debt?
Love, can it hit one without hitting two and leave
  the one lost and groping?
Love, can you pick it up like a mouse and put it in
  your pocket and take it to your room and bring it
  out of your pocket and say,
        O here is my love,
        my little pretty mousey love?

          ::

    Yes—love, this little word you hear about,
      is love an elephant and you step out of the way
      where the elephant comes trampling, tromping,
      traveling with big feet and long flaps of
      drooping ears and straight white ivory tusks—
      and you step out of the way with respect,
      with high respect, and surprise near to shock
      as you say,
          Dear God, he's big,
          big like stupendous is big,
          heavy and elephantine and funny,
          immense and slow and easy.
    I'm asking, is love an elephant?

Or could it be love is a snake—like a rattlesnake,
  like a creeping winding slithering rattlesnake
  with fangs—poison fangs they tell me,
  and when the bite of it gets you
  then you run crying for help
  if you don't fall cold and dead on the way.
Can love be a snake?

Or would you say love is a flamingo, with pink feathers—
  a soft sunset pink, a sweet gleaming naked pink—
  and with enough long pink feathers
  you could make the fan for a fan dance
  and hear a girl telling her lover,
    Speak, my chosen one,
    and give me your wish
    as to what manner of fan dance
    you would have from me
    in the cool of evening
    or the black velvet sheen of midnight.
Could it be love is a flamingo?

Or is love a big red apple, and you don't know
  whether to bite into it—and you knock on wood
  and call off your luck numbers and hold your breath—
  and you put your teeth into it and get a mouthful,
  tasting all there is to it,
  and whether it's sweet and wild
  or a dry mush you want to spit out,
  it's something else than you expected.
I'm asking, sir, is love a big red apple?

Or maybe love is goofer dust, I hadn't thought about that—
  for you go to the goofer tree at midnight
  and gather the leaves and crush them into fine dust,
  very fine dust, sir, and when your man sleeps
  you sprinkle it in his shoes and he's helpless

and from then on he can't get away from you,
    he's snared and tangled and can't keep from loving you.
Could goofer dust be the answer?

And I've heard some say love is a spy and a sneak,
    a blatherer, a gabby mouth,
    tattling and tittering as it tattles,
    and you believe it and take it to your heart
    and nurse it like good news,
    like heaven-sent news meant for you
    and you only—precious little you.
Have you heard love comes creeping and cheating like that?

::

And are they after beguiling and befoozling us
    when they tell us love is a rose, a red red rose,
    the mystery of leaves folded over and under
    and you can take it to pieces and throw it away
    petal by petal into the wind blowing it away
    or you can wear it for a soft spot of crimson
    in your hair, at your breast,
    and you can waltz and tango wearing your sweet crimson rose
    and take it home and lay it on a window sill and see it
    wither brown, curl black, and shrivel
    until one day you're not careful
    and it crackles into dust in your hand
    and the wind whisks it whither you know not,
    whither you care not,
    for it is just one more flame of a rose
    that came with its red blush and crimson bloom
    and did the best it could with what it had
    and nobody wins, nobody loses,
    and what's one more rose
    when on any street corner
    in bright summer mornings

you see them with bunches of roses,
their hands out toward you calling,
> Roses today, fresh roses,
> fresh-cut roses today
> a rose for you sir,
> the ladies like roses,
> now is the time,
> fresh roses sir.

And I'm waiting—for days and weeks and months
I've been waiting to see some flower seller,
one of those hawkers of roses,
I've been waiting to hear one of them calling,
> A cabbage with every rose,
> a good sweet cabbage with every rose,
> a head of cabbage for soup or slaw or stew,
> cabbage with the leaves folded over
> and under like a miracle
> and you can eat it and stand up and walk,
> today and today only your last chance
> a head of cabbage with every single lovely rose.
And any time and any day I hear a flower seller so calling
I shall be quick and I shall buy
two roses and two cabbages,
the roses for my lover
and the cabbages for little luckless me.
Or am I wrong—is love a rose you can buy and give away
and keep for yourself cabbages, my lord and master,
cabbages, kind sir?
I am asking, can you?

And it won't help any, it won't get us anywhere,
it won't wipe away what has been
nor hold off what is to be,
if you hear me saying
love is a little white bird

and the flight of it so fast
you can't see it
and you know it's there
only by the faint whirr of its wings
and the hush song coming so low to your ears
you fear it might be silence
and you listen keen and you listen long
and you know it's more than silence
for you get the hush song so lovely
it hurts and cuts into your heart
and what you want is to give more than you can get
and you'd like to write it but it can't be written
and you'd like to sing it but you don't dare try
because the little white bird sings it better than you can
so you listen and while you listen you pray
and after you pray you meditate, then pray more
and one day it's as though a great slow wind
had washed you clean and strong inside and out
and another day it's as though you had gone to sleep
in an early afternoon sunfall and your sleeping heart
dumb and cold as a round polished stone,
and the little white bird's hush song
telling you nothing can harm you,
the days to come can weave in and weave out
and spin their fabrics and designs for you
and nothing can harm you—
unless you change yourself into a thing of harm
nothing can harm you.

::

The little white bird is my candidate.
Ladies and gentlemen, I give you
the little white bird you can't see
though you can hear its hush song
and when you hear that hush song it's love

and I'm ready to swear to it—
you can bring in a stack of affidavits
and I'll swear to it and sign my name
to every last one, so help me God.
And if a fat bumbling shopworn court clerk tells me,
Hold up your hand, I'll hold up my hand all right
and when he bumbles and mumbles to me like I was
one more witness it was work for him to give the oath to,
when he blabs, You do solemnly swear so help you God
that in this cause you will tell the truth,
the whole truth and nothing but the truth,
I'll say to him, I do, and I'll say to myself,
And no thanks to you and you could be more immaculate
with the name of God.

> I am done.
> I have finished.
> I give you the little white bird—
> and my thanks for your hearing me—
> > and my prayers for you,
> > my deep silent prayers.

OFFERING AND REBUFF

I could love you
as dry roots love rain.
I could hold you
as branches in the wind
brandish petals.
Forgive me for speaking
so soon.

: :

Let your heart look
on white sea spray
and be lonely.

Love is a fool star.

You and a ring of stars
may mention my name
and then forget me.

Love is a fool star.

: :

MORNING GLORY BLUE

The blue of morning glory climbs fences and houses.
It is a Gettysburg Union blue setting itself against
   a morning haze.

The blue of morning glory spots and spatters a rail
   fence.
The fence zigzags and the morning glory staggers on
   a path of sea-blue, sky-blue, Gettysburg Union
   blue.

HIGH MOMENTS

Keep this flower to remember me by.
        So she told him.
Keep this, remember me, remember.
Fold this flower where you never forget.
Put me by where time no longer counts.
Then come back to a sure remembering.

  Night itself, night is one long dark flower.
She said night knows deep rememberings,
All flowers being some kind of remembering
    And night itself folding up like
            many smooth dark flowers.

    Find me like the night finds.
    She measured herself so.
    Keep me like the night keeps
    For I have night deeps in me.

    Flesh is a doom and a prison.
    Flesh jails those only flesh.
      Air speaks nevertheless,
    spray, fire, air,
    thin voices beyond capture
    save only in remembering
    the luster of lost stars,
    the reach for a wafer of moon.

    Let us talk it over long
    and wear cream gold buttons
    and be proud we have anger and pride together,
    remembering high loveliness hovers in time
    and is made of passing moments.

    I have kept high moments.
    They go round and round in me.

MUMMY

Blood is blood and bone is bone.
All bloods are red and all bones white.
The beginning is being born.
The end is being dead.
    The magnificent repeated themes of line and color
    forming the final exterior of a Pharaoh mummy
    try to appeal otherwise and fix an affirmation
    of the blood there yet and the bones there yet.
Nevertheless and for all the exquisite patterning
The blood is dry as dust and the bones obey no voices
Telling them to rise and walk.

Some such Pharaohs are born with a name,
one more of a line of names.
Some such Pharaohs die with music and mourning
and sleep under careful epitaphs.
Yet they and the scrubs, the rabble, the hoi polloi
end in the same democracy to never fail them all,
to be true to each, to render the blood and bones
of high and humble the dust of homage.
This is the timeworn chant of the grand democrat
Death: dust to dust, ashes to ashes.
For them all, scrub or wellborn, the hustle, the race,
the hullabaloo, is over.
They no longer earn their livings.
They no longer take what is handed them.

OLD HOKUSAI PRINT

In a house he remembers in the Howlong valley
not far from bends of the Shooshoo river
where each of the leaves of fall
is a pigeon foot of gold on the blue:
there is a house of a thousand windows
and in every window the same woman
and she too remembers better than she forgets:
she too has one wish for every window:
   and the mountains forty miles away
   rise and fade, come and go,
   in lights and mist there and not there,
   beckoning as mountains seen on a Monday,
   phantoms traveled away on a Tuesday,
   scrawls in a dim blot on Wednesday,
   gone into grey shawls on Friday,
   lost and found in half lavenders often,
   back again one day saying they were not gone,
   not gone at all, being merely unseen,
the white snow on the blue peaks no dream snow,
no dream at all the sawtooth line of purple garments.
Can a skyline share itself like drums in the heart?

ONE PARTING

Why did he write to her,
"I can't live with you"?
And why did she write to him,
"I can't live without you"?
For he went west, she went east,
And they both lived.

EVER A SEEKER

The fingers turn the pages.
The pages unfold as a scroll.
There was the time there was no America.
Then came on the scroll an early
    America, a land of beginnings,
    an American being born.
Then came a later America, seeker
    and finder, yet ever more seeker
    than finder, ever seeking its way
    amid storm and dream.

OLD MUSIC FOR QUIET HEARTS

Be still as before oh pool
Be blue and still oh pool
As before blue   as before still
Oh pool of the many communions

A wingprint may come
Flash over and be gone
    A yellow leaf may fall
    May sink and join
    Companion fallen leaves
The print of blue sky
The night bowl of stars
These far off pass and bypass
Over you blue   over you still
Oh pool of the many communions

Now hold your quiet glass oh pool
Now keep your mirrorlight blue
    They come and they go
    And one and all
    You know them one and all
    And they know not you
Nor you nor your mirrorlight blue
Only old music for quiet hearts.

PERSONALIA

The personal idiom of a corn shock satisfies me.

So does the attack of a high note by an Australian mezzo-soprano.

Also the face and body blow punishment taken by the boilermaker who won the world's championship belt.

I find majesty in the remembrance of a stump speech by John P. Altgeld explaining his act as governor of Illinois in the pardon of four convicts.

The simple dignity of a child drinking a bowl of milk embodies the fascination of an ancient rite.

The color of redhaws when the last driving rain of October sprays their gypsy crimson against the khaki brown of the blown leaves, the ankle-deep leaves—

If I should be sent to jail I would write of these things, lover of mine.

If I live to a majestic old age becoming the owner of a farm I shall sit under apple trees in the summer and on a pad of paper with a large yellow lead pencil, I shall write of these things, lover of mine.

THE GONG OF TIME

Time says hush.
　By the gong of time you live.
　Listen and you hear time saying you were silent
　　　long before you came to life and you will
　　　again be silent long after you leave it,
　　　why not be a little silent now?
　　　　　　Hush yourself, noisy little man.

Time hushes all.
　The gong of time rang for you to come out of a
　　　hush and you were born.
　The gong of time will ring for you to go back to
　　　the same hush you came from.
　Winners and losers, the weak and the strong, those
　　　who say little and try to say it well, and
　　　those who babble and prattle their lives away,
　　　　　Time hushes all.

PRAIRIE WOODLAND

Yellow leaves speak early November's heart on the river.
Winding in prairie woodland the curves of the water course
    are a young woman's breasts.
Flutter and flutter go the spear shapes—it is a rust and a
    saffron always dropping hour on hour.
Sunny and winey the filtering shine of air passes the drivers,
    cornhuskers, farmers, children in the fields.
Red jags of sumach and slashes of shag-bark hickory are a crim-
    son and gray cramming pictures on the river glass.
Out of their tubes of May and June they squeeze great changing
    dabs of earth love, wind passion.
Now it is a sorrel horse neck, now a slow fire of Warsaw, any-
    thing you wish for—here in the moving leaves and slow
    waters.
Five o'clock and a lemon sky—long tubes spread lemon miles and
    miles—submarines, dreadnaughts, coal-boats, flotillas of
    destroyers cross the lemon sea bringing darkness, night.

SHADOWS FALL BLUE ON THE MOUNTAINS

Shadows fall blue on the mountains.
Mountains fall gray to the rivers.
Rivers fall winding to the sea.
Oldest of all the blue creep,
          the gray crawl of the sea
And only shadows falling older than the sea.

::

Can you begin to own
both yourself and your shadow?
Can you measure
moments in the sun
when your shadow lays down your shape?
Does your shadow speak to you
or is it you telling your shadow
what to be telling you?
Can a man listen to his shadow
hoping it tells him where to go,
what to do when he gets there?
Has ever been a man praying,
  "Make me into a thin
    goblet of glass, oh Lord.
I fear what my shadow tells me"?
What has happened
when you forget and the sun forgets
to lay down your old companion,
        your lifelong shadow?

::

Now the shadow of Shakespeare—
what did he say to it?
what did he leave unsaid?
and how well did he know he left
     millions of shadow soliloquies unspoken?

When Napoleon saw his shadow
could it be he lacked for words
and often beyond his own
saw shadows fateful as his own?

: :

Shadows lighter than any mist
fall on the sea's blue creep,
     on the sea's gray crawl.

Fateful high over
swings the sun
swings the High Witness
     of shadows.

QUOTATIONS

Said the panama hat to the fedora:
"Sins have different prices in hell."
Said the fedora hat to the panama:
"Yeah, nickel and dime sins, silver-dollar sins,
sins setting you back a century, a grand,
sins you can't settle under a million bucks,
tin and aluminum sins, brass sins, copper, old gold,
pint and bushel sins, inch and mile sins,
calculated little teapot sins and roaring tornadoes."

SKYSCRAPERS STAND PROUD

The skyscrapers stand proud.
They seem to say they have
    sought the absolute
    and made it their own.
Yet they are blameless, innocent
    as dumb steel and the dumber
    concrete of their bastions.
"Man made us," they murmur. "We are
    proud only as man is proud and we
    have no more found the absolute
    than has man."

POOL OF BETHESDA

A man came to the pool of Bethesda
and sat down for his thoughts.
The light of the sun ran through the line
of the water and struck where the moss on
a stone was green—
The green of the moss wove into the sun silver
and the silent brackets of seven prisms added
to the pool of Bethesda—
Thus a man sat long with a pool and its prisms.

. .

FIRST SONATA FOR KARLEN PAULA

At an autumn evening bonfire
came rose-candle co-ordinations.
  Burning and burnt
came a slow song of fire leaves.

  The summer brought
valley breaths of spun moonmist.

  Can there be keys
commanding the locks of constellations,
letting loose white spokes of light,
             blue waves of flame?

        . .

  Make like before, sweet child.
Be you like five new oranges in a wicker basket.
  Step out like
a summer evening fireworks over black waters.
  Be dizzy in a haze of yellow silk bandannas.
Then in a change of costume
        sit silent in a chair of tarnished bronze
Having spoken with a grave mouth:
              "Now I will be
              a clavichord melody
              in October brown.
              You will see me in
              deep-sea contemplation
              on a yellow horse in a white wind."

    . .

Her room had a number.
Likewise she had a number.
They heard her saying:
"Who is more numbers than I am?
Which of you on a golden morning
has sent a silver bullet
into a crimson target?"

. .

Daybreak creeps
in a first thin shimmering.
  Neither is the day come
  nor the night gone.

. .

Be shabbawobba now
before this pool of day to come.
    Speak and be still.
    Listen and be still.
A ring of topaz floats in rose-light.
Handles of moongold go in a hush.
The pool welcomes a pair of orange slippers,
the gauze of them winking out and coming back.
Come passwords, come numerals,
              come changing altar lights.
Fingers, be cool, strum only half-heard chords.
Let your words be softer than
    a slow south wind blowing thistledown.

THOU ART LIKE A FLOWER

"Thou art like a flower,"
Ran an old song line.
What flower did he mean?
She might have been a quiet blue flower.
She wore crimson carnations perhaps.
She may have planted tall sunflowers
Stooping with hollyhocks around a kitchen doorstep.
They may have picked bluebells together
Or talked about wild arbutus they found.
Perhaps she knew what he meant by telling her:
"Thou art like a flower."

SOLO FOR SATURDAY NIGHT GUITAR

Time was. Time is. Time shall be.
Man invented time to be used.
Love was. Love is. Love shall be.
Yet man never invented love
Nor is love to be used like time.
A clock wears numbers one to twelve
And you look and read its face
And tell the time pre-cise-ly ex-act-ly.
Yet who reads the face of love?
Who tells love numbers pre-cise-ly ex-act-ly?
Holding love in a tight hold for keeps,
Fastening love down and saying
"It's here now and here for always."
You don't do this offhand, careless-like.
Love costs. Love is not so easy
Nor is the shimmering of star dust
Nor the smooth flow of new blossoms
Nor the drag of a heavy hungering for someone.
  Love is a white horse you ride
  or wheels and hammers leaving you lonely
  or a rock in the moonlight for rest
  or a sea where phantom ships cross always
  or a tall shadow always whispering
  or a circle of spray and prisms—
  maybe a rainbow round your shoulder.
    Heavy heavy is love to carry
    and light as one rose petal,
    light as a bubble, a blossom,
    a remembering bar of music
    or a finger or a wisp of hair
    never forgotten.

ROSE BAWN

She believed herself to have gone through tall gateways
and to have marched triumphant across fire and thorn.
She sat in front of a county building, under a mulberry,
and once she mumbled to an invisible Irish sweetheart,
"All the knocking of the tumblers of the sea is in my
knee bones."

When the chariots of thunder drove and rolled overhead,
she mumbled, "When the water comes through the sieve of
the sky, that makes the rain—God does it easy—God does
all things easy."

Memories swept over her like a strong wind on dark waters.
She half-whispered, "When the moongold came on the water
afterward it was too much money—too much by far—more than
we wanted."

SPEECH

There was
what we call "words,"
a lot of language,
syllables,
each syllable made of air.

Then there was
s i l e n c e ,
no talk at all,
no more syllables
shaped by living tongues
out of wandering air.

Thus all tongues
slowly talk themselves
into s i l e n c e .

RUNAWAY COLORS

The smoke of these landscapes has gone God knows where.
The sun touches them off with shot gold of an evening,
  with a mother's grey eyes singing to her children.
The blue smudge on a haystack a mile off is gone God knows
  where.
The yellow dust of a sheet over Emil Hawkinson's cornfield,
The ribbons of red picked at by the high-flying hard-crying
  crows,
These too are in the pits of the west God knows where.

OUT OF THE RAINBOW END

For Edward Steichen

A delphinium flings a shadow
with a rooted stalk—
   a personal shadow.
   Each silhouette documents
   designs and dooms woven
   between shape and shadowshape.

You may add two delphiniums
with seeds lighted in soil
with stalks prepared in loam
toward the upheave into bloom
when stalk and leaves find a path
hold a rocketform of blue
hold it in a velvet stillstand.

In a summer daybreak rain
a huddle of delphiniums
across spikes of fogblue leaves
out of little mistblue cups
   trade meditations on being
   shapes and shadowshapes.

Cups and bells nod in the sun,
in the fine dust of the wind:
one newborn delphinium laughing
at the long scroll of marriages
   whereby she is the latest child
   bringing to the bright air her shape,
   to the dark earth her shadow.

Shaded out of seven prisms
in choices by living fingers
out of the rainbow end?
   Yes and the winds
   of many evenings came:
dawns drew in with dew and mist
and the bells of many rains rang.
               Soft and lovely
               these transients go yet stay
               Even their violence goes in velvet.

SUN DANCER

Spider, you have long silver legs.
You may spin diagrams of doom.
Your patterns may throw fine glints
Festooned from wandering silk.
It may be neither art nor money
Nor calisthenics nor engineering.
No man trusts any woman and vice versa.
All men love all women and vice versa.
And all friends cherish each other.
And there are triflers who flirt with death.
Spider, you have long silver legs.

THEMES IN CONTRAST

A blue shot dawn,
A white shot dawn,
And she went out.

Into the dawn water
Until the dawn water
Came over her head.

And she came back
Out of the water
Into a blue shot dawn,
Into a white shot dawn.

: :

The trucks and the cavalry came,
The shoes and the wheels, the tarpaulins
    dripping.
And the shadows of the grain elevators
In the hump of the blown white moon,
And the breathing of the tugs and barges
In the change of the fog river gray—
These all crossed over; the day after they
    stood up; the day after was something
    else again.

TWO FISH

when the two fish spoke
their speech was scarlet

    they met in a bowl
    of molten gold air

    they swung in an arch
    of seven rainbow sheens

    they swam in a grotto
    one of a thousand grottoes

    they shook their fins
    in a green feather dust

SMOKE SHAPES

Egg Faces

Lights of egg faces, lights of monkey skulls,
meet each other, meet yourselves.
Lights of the morning sun warming the night-
wet wood, fires of far-back mornings fixing
your caldrons cooling to firestone,
meet each other, meet yourselves.
Sheet white egg faces, strong and sad gorilla
mugs, meet yourselves, meet each other.

Long Heads

Sleep, long-face of the long-head family.
Go back to the inside of the ten thousandth
mountain you came from.
Out of sleep you came; back to sleep you go.

Eyes out of morning twilights, how now it is easy
to join up with evening twilights.
Nose cut from the spear handle of a morning star
finding its mirror-slant in a mountain rock nose,
how now it is easy to sit next and alongside an
evening star spear handle.
Yearn, too; you might as well yearn; yearners or
not, out of sleep, back to sleep; this is put on
the mouth.
Sleep, long-face, back now to the inside of the
ten thousandth mountain.

THREE SHRINES

Three shrines a woman has for a man.
She loves him for what he is out in the world.
She loves him for what he seems to her of which
    the world knows nothing.
She loves him for the touch of his personal
    magnets.
Thus we might frame these three declarations and
    listen to bystanders:

               Is that so?
               Who told you—a little bird?
               What are these personal magnets?
               What is a shrine?
               You mean she never opened
                   a barrel of snakes for him?

VARIATIONS ON A THEME

She was given crystal flesh for a home.
And her windows were tremulous to visions.
Love me, love me, was her often cry.
She put lover higher than all else.
She carried series of love-birds and gave away.

::

Pour love deep into me.
Thus ran her cry.
Let me have all love.
She murmured this want.
Love may be toil, waste, death
Yet come pour love deep into me.
Thus her years ran to one theme.

TIMESWEEP

I was born in the morning of the world,
So I know how morning looks,
   morning in the valley wanting,
   morning on a mountain wanting.
Morning looks like people look,
   like a cornfield wanting corn,
   like a sea wanting ships.
Tell me about any strong beautiful wanting
   And there is your morning, my morning,
       everybody's morning.

Makers and givers may be moon shaken,
         may be star lost,
Knowing themselves as sea-deep seekers,
         both seeking and sought,
Knowing love is a ring and the ring endless,
Seeing love as a wheel and the wheel endless.

     Love may be a hard flesh crying its want.
     Love may be a thin horizon air,
     thinner than snowwhite wool finespun,
     finer than any faint blue mist
     blown away and gone on yesterday's wind.

      There are hungers
      for a nameless bread
      out of the dust
      of the hard earth,
      out of the blaze
      of the calm sun.

Blow now, winds, you so old at blowing.
Oak at the river, pine at the rocks,
 brandish your arms
Slow to a whisper wind, fast to a storm howl.

:: :

The wind carves sand into shapes,
Endless the fresh designs,
Wind and ice patient beyond telling.
Ice can tip mountains over,
Ice the giant beyond measure.
And the sun governs valley lights,
Transforms hats into shoes and back again
Before we are through any long looking.

:: :

The pink nipples of the earth in springtime,
The long black eyelashes of summer's look,
The harvest laughter of tawny autumn,
The winter silence of land in snow covers,
Each speaks its own oaths of the cool and the flame
 of naked possessions clothed and come naked again:
  The sea knows it all.
  They all crept out of the sea.

:: :

These wheels within wheels
These leaves folded in leaves
These wheeling winds
 and winding leaves
Those sprockets
 from those seeds
This spiral shooting
 from that rainfall—

What does a turning earth
    say to its axis?
How should a melon say thanks
Or a squash utter blessings?

        : :

In the heave of the hankering sea
God put precisions of music and accord
to be heard in the deepest seabells
amid the farthest violet spawn
moving in seagreen doom and skyblue promise.
    The sea shares its tokens—
        how and with whom?

To these shores birds return
    and keep returning
for the curves of fresh flights.
To these waters fish return
    and keep returning
for the fathoming of old waters.
To sky and sea they are born
and keep returning to be reborn.

The sharing of the sea goes on
for the sake of wings and fins
ever returning to new skyblue,
ever reborn in new seagreen.

Could the gray-green lobster speak
    what would he say
    of personal secrets?
Could one white gull utter a word—
    what would it be?
    what white feather of a word?

     : :

Among the shapes and shadow-shapes
in the blurs of the marching animals,
among the open forms, the hidden and half-hidden,
who is the Head One? Me? Man?
Am I first over all, I the genus homo?

Where did I come from?
How doing now and where to from here?
Is there any going back?
And where might I want to go back?
Is it told in my dreams and hankerings, looking
back at what I was, seeing what I am?
Like so a man talking to himself
of the bitter, the sweet, the bittersweet:
he had heard likenings of himself:
Cock of the walk, brave as a lion, fierce as a tiger,
Stubborn as a mule, mean as a louse, crazy as a bedbug,
Soft as a kitten, slimy as an octopus, one poor fish.

Then he spoke for himself:
I am bat-eyed, chicken-hearted, monkey-faced.
Listen and you'll hear it told,
I am a beast out of the jungle.
Man, proud man, with a peacock strut
seeing himself in his own man-made mirrors.
Yet I am myself all the animals.
Mix in among lavender shadows the gorilla far back
And the jungle cry of readiness for death
Or struggle—and the clean breeds who live on
In the underbrush. Mix in farther back yet
Breeds out of the slime of the sea.
Put in a high green of a restless sea.
Insinuate chlorine and mystic salts,
The make-up of vertebrates,
the long highway of mammals who chew
Their victims and feed their children

From milk at a breast,
The fathers and the mothers who battled hunger
And tore each other's jugulars
Over land and women, laughter and language.
Put in mystery without end. Then add mystery.
   The memorandum runs long.
   I have feet, fins and wings.
   I live on land, in the sea, in the air.
   I run, fly, sneak, prowl, I kill and eat.
   Among killers and eaters I am first.
   I am the Head One.

What is this load I carry out of yesterday?
What are these bygones of dreams, moans, shadows?
What jargons, what gibberish, must I yet unlearn?

I have been a dim plasm in the sea,
rocking dumb, not-so-dumb, dumb again,
   a dab and a dangling tangle
   swarming and splitting to live again.

I have been a drop of jelly
   aching with a silver shot of light
      and it sang Be-now Now-be Be-now Now-be.

I have been a rockabye baby
sloshed in the sludge of the sea
and I have clung with a shell over me
waiting a tide to bring me breakfast.

I have been the little fish eaten by the big one
and I have been the big fish
taking ten lesser fish in one fast gulp.

I have been a shrimp, one of a billion,
fed to a million little fish
ending as fodder in the bellies of big fish.

In the seven seas
of the one vast glumbering sea over the globe
I have been eater and eaten,
toiler and hanger-on.

I lived half in the sea, half on land,
swimmer and crawler, fins and legs.

I traveled with layers of earthworms
grinding limestone into loam.

Encased as a snail
I wrought one pure spiral,
an image of no beginning, no end.
"This is the image wherein I live;
the outer form of me to be here
when the dried inner one drifts
away into thin air."

I have journeyed
for sticks and mud and weaving thongs
to build me a home in a bush.

I have mounted into the blue sky
with a mate lark on a summer morning,
dropping into sycamore branches to warble.

The orioles called me one of theirs;
herons taught me to stand and wait in marsh grass,
to preen my wings and rise with legs bundled behind.

    I was the awkward pelican
    flying low along the florida coast with a baby.

    I stood with pink flamingoes
    in long lagoons at tallahassee watching sunrise.

I am black as a crow with a *caw-caw* in my throat
and I am lush with morning calls of catbird and mocker,
the cardinal's *what-cheer what-cheer*
and the redbird's whistle across hemlock timbers
in early april in wisconsin.

I have done the cleansing service
of scavengers on land and sea;
the red and sea-green lobsters told me
how they win a living.
I have slunk among buzzards and broken hunger
with a beak in a rottening horse.
I have fed where my greatgrandfathers fed.

I know the faint half-words
of the fly and the flea,
the midge, the mosquito.
I was kin of a vampire
doing what a blind thirst told me.
A louse seeking red blood told me
I carry feeders in blood.

I ganged up with maggots
and cleaned a cadaver
and left the bones gleaming.

I am a grasshopper taking in one jump
a hundred grasshopper lengths.
I buzz with earnest bees
in the lingering sun of apple orchards.
I loiter with tumble bugs
seeming to know solemn causes.
I climb with spiders, throw ladders, nets,
frameworks out of my navel coils.
I am the building ant
of architectonic galleries and chambers.

I am egg, cocoon and moth.
I count my caterpillar rings of black and yellow.
I inch with the inch worms
measuring pearl-green miles of summer months.
I have swept in the ashen paths of weevils,
borers, chinch bugs eating their way.
Born once as a late morning child
I died of old age before noon.
Or again I issued as a luna moth,
circles of gold spotting my lavender wings.
I have zigzagged with blue water bugs
among white lotus and pond lilies.
From my silver throat in the dew of evening
came a whippoorwill call, one, another, more
as a slow gold moon told time with climbing.

I am the chameleon taking the tint of what I live on,
the water frog green as the scum he sits on,
the tree frog gray as the tree-bark-gray.
The duck, the swan, the goose, met me as sisters,
the beaver, the porcupine, the chinchilla, as brothers.
The rattlesnakes let me live with them
to eat mice, to salivate birds and rabbits
and fatten in sleep on noontime rocks.
I was a lizard, a texas horned toad,
a centipede counting my century of legs.
I was a crocodile in africa
with a lazy mouthful of teeth.

The stealth of the rat, the mink, the squirrel, came.
The weasel gave me his lingo
of now-you-see-me now-you-don't.
The rabbit hide-out in clover, the gopher hole,
the mole tunnel, the corn-shock nest of the mouse,
these were a few of my homes.

One summer night with fireflies
I too was fluttering night gold.

Long ago I ran with the eohippus,
the little horse that was.
I wore dodo feathers
but that's all passed.
I had a feathered form fade in fog:
you can find it now in feathered fossils.
I was a mammoth, a dinosaur
and other hulks too big to last.
I have been more quadrupeds than I can name.
I was the son of a wild jackass
with swift and punishing heels.
I lifted my legs and carried a camel hump
in slow caravans pausing at nightfall,
lifting my hump again at dawn.

I locked my horns with another moose;
our antlers lie locked and our bones whitening.

I slouched up hills of ice with polar bears,
practiced smell with the red fox,
trained my fangs with timber wolves.
I fight now for the rights to a carcass.
The killer who crouches, gets set, and leaps
is a kinsman I can call my cousin.
The strangling gibberish of the gorilla
comes out of my anxious mouth.
Among a thousand ring-tailed monkeys
scratching buttocks, sharing fleas,
shinning up trees in guatemala, I am one.
Among the blue-rumped baboons,
chattering chimpanzees and leering orangoutangs,
I am at home using paws for hands, hands for paws.
The howl of one hyena eating another is mine.

In a boneless tube of ooze
I soaked dumb days with sponges
off the gulfcoast sea-bottom.
Now I am the parrot
who picks up palaver and repeats it.
Now I am the river-hog, the hippopotamus
and I am the little bird who lives in his ear
and tells him when to get up and where to go.
I took a long sweet time learning to talk
and now I carry many half-words not yet made,
hankering hoodoo words taking shape in mud:
protoplasm, spermatozoa, phantasms, taboos.
In the pour of a thrush morningsong,
in the lonesome cry of a loon at moonrise,
is the rush of more half-words:

All horns are one horn
and I am the sheep, the goat,
the yak, the buffalo, the prongbuck.

All shells are one shell
and I am the mussel clam,
the oyster, the mother-of-pearl.

I have been a freshwater polyp, a star-fish,
budding into evermore births of likeness
following likeness.

I have spent nights as kin of singing crickets,
meadow locusts, katydids, only the males singing,
the females silent and waiting.

I have been the calling frog with a bubble at his
throat—and the spotted snake who came to spell
doom and appeasement of hunger.

I have spoken as a brother to the walking stick
and the hesitations of his stilts and knee-joints.

I am the penguin and ostrich
trying to remember lost wings.
    I am the snake who had many legs
    trying to remember my lost legs.

        I have had a thousand fish faces, sea faces,
          sliding off into land faces, monkey faces—
            I began in a dim green mist
                    of floating faces.

I have worn covers of thick strong hair and smooth fur.
I have shed rain and sleet with my feathers and down.
I have carried thick wool wrapping me warm as I slept in snow.
I have had tropic and arctic garments bestowed on me.

                                    : :

Since death is there in the light of the sun, in the song of the wind,
Since death is there in the marvel of the sun coming up to travel its
    arc and go down saying, "I am time and you are time,"
Since death is there in the slow creep of every dawn and in all the
    steps of shadow moving into evening and dusk of stars,
Since death is there in almost inaudible chimes of every slow clocktick
    beginning at the birth hour there must be a tremor of music in
    the last little gong, the pling of the final announcement from the
    Black Void.

Have I not seen forms
flowing into faces and voices—
numbers hoarse and high with the mating cry
over rolling white sea-horses and forked lightning,
over the infinite velvet of blue land-fog,
over sacramental bread and heavy blood roses,

over mate-brown pigeons flying into burnt wilderness,
gazing into star-pool waters holding the great serene
                              constellations?

I meditate with the mud eel
on where we came from.
Not yet can I give the scream speech
of a great white albatross—
frozen foam and sea-drift for her
high on an iceberg's shining white hat,
whirr and sweep of her wings
in the splinters of an arc of northern lights.

I am a three-hundred-year-old galapagos turtle,
sleeping and eating, eating and sleeping,
blinking and easy, sleepy-eyed and easy,
while shakespeare writes a flock of plays,
while john bunyan sits in jail and writes a book,
while cromwell, napoleon, lincoln, wilson, lenin,
      come and go, stride and vanish,
while bryan, morgan, rockefeller, lafollette, altgeld,
      become names spelled and written.
I sleep, forget, remember, forget again, and ask:
      What of it?
      Don't bother me, brother.
      Don't bother a dozing turtle
      born to contemplate and yawn.

I was a scorpion and a tarantula
before the first huts of guadalajara,
before the first aztecs gathered bananas.
I was a maroon cockatoo and a green parakeet
before the first incas fashioned bird-cages.
In western nebraska I was a wild prairie pony
with a white forelock down my sorrel face

before ever a caesar or alexander or any czar
dreamed the smoke-shadow of a dream
of shattering armies beyond the horizon
                              and taking over.

What is this burden I carry out of yesterday?
Why am I so wise, so grand, so cunning, so ignorant?
What have I made that I haven't broken?
What have I bred that I haven't killed?
Why have I prized my skills as a killer?
What jargons, what gibberish, must I yet unlearn?
What are these bygones of dreams, moans, shadows?
Who are these people I come from who follow the ways
of long-gone time and long-gone fathers?

    What are these bygones
    sea-brought and land-locked?
For I am one and all of them:
they swarm in me with song, cry and murmur;
they fill my room with scurrying fish,
with apes and kangaroos, with swine and birds;
they bring arenas and theaters of action
wherein they kill, eat, crave, sing, live on,
or perish before the might of the stronger;
they stir with bleats and moans;
they fade with growls and chuckles.

They dream in me
and rise dripping on sea horizons
to shout hosannahs, to cry thanks,
to vanish leaving no sign nor track
on the silent lines of green mist.

    The earth rocked me
    in a cradle of winds.

The fog and the mud
clung as a wrap and home
of swaddling cloths.
And the sea sang bye-lo bye-lo
and the stars and the rains
brought changing songs: so-long so-long
joined to the sea's old bye-lo bye-lo.

.

Deep roots moving in lush soil to send a silver-gray beech tree straight
toward the sky—
Shallow roots in barren land sending their stalks of grass and weeds up
over to bend in the wind with whisper tones—
Tangled and winding roots in desert wastes rising into cactus and the
joshua tree to bring a hush on the air with spare and murmuring
blossoms wrought from dews of night air—
Am I, are you, kin to these everliving roots? Have you, have I, one
time long ago been an oak with a wind song in our leaves?
Have the bones of your torso spoken low to a sugar maple in october
flaming in branch and leaf: "We can not be strangers, I know how
you are what you are in root and trunk."

::

I have said to the elephant and the flea, "Each of us makes his life
in what to him is the Known and for each of us there is a vast
Unknown and farther beyond the vaster Unknowable—and the
Ignorance we share and share alike is immeasurable."
The one-eyed mollusc on the sea-bottom, feathered and luminous, is
my equal in what he and I know of star clusters not yet found by
the best of star-gazers.

::

The earth is a forgotten cinder.
A heaving fireball cooled off.
Thus the story of the rocks.
Each river came later than the cooling.
Next comes the freezing of the globe.
A heaving iceball will travel alone.
The rivers will be too cold to move.
Each flowering valley will be a memory.
The autobiography of a wild rose will run:
My leaves pressed between the times
                    of a fireball and an iceball.

::

I have been woven among meshes of long ropes
and fine filaments: older than the rocks and
fresh as the dawn of this morning today are
the everliving roots who begot me,
who poured me as one more seeker
one more swimmer in the gold and gray procession
of phantoms laughing, fighting, singing, moan-
ing toward the great cool calm of the fixed
return to the filaments of dust.

I am more than a traveler out of Nowhere.
Sea and land, sky and air, begot me Somewhere.
Where I go from here and now, or if I go at all
    again, the Maker of sea and land, of sky and
    air, can tell.

::

There is only one horse on the earth
and his name is All Horses.

There is only one bird in the air
and his name is All Wings.
There is only one fish in the sea
and his name is All Fins.
There is only one man in the world
and his name is All Men.
There is only one woman in the world
and her name is All Women.
There is only one child in the world
and the child's name is All Children.

    There is only one Maker in the world
    and His children cover the earth
    and they are named All God's Children.